FISHING

Gary Newman

with thanks to Selena Masson

CLASH

by ticktock

First published in Great Britain in 2008 by ticktock Media Ltd,
2 Orchard Business Centre, North Farm Road, Tunbridge Wells, Kent, TN2 3XF

project editor and picture researcher: Ruth Owen
ticktock project designer: Sara Greasley

With thanks to series editors Honor Head and Jean Coppendale,
www.theessentialfly.co.uk and www.flyfishingusa.com.

Thank you to Lorraine Petersen and the members of nasen

ISBN 978 1 84696 716 0 pbk

Printed in China

Picture credits (t=top; b=bottom; c=centre; l=left; r=right):
age fotostock/ SuperStock: 17b. J. L. Allworks: 13t, 13c. J. L. Allworks / The Essential Fly: 19. Angling Times: 1, 4t.
BilderLounge/ SuperStock: 24-25. Ian Chapman: 8c, 10. Chad Ehlers/ Alamy: 22l. Henry Gilbey: 2-3, 5, 14-15, 17t,
18t. Simon Grosset/ Alamy: 22r. IGFA (International Game Fish Association): 31. Steve Lockett: 26-27, 28, 29. Roy
Morsch/CORBIS: OFC. George Shelley/CORBIS: 18b. Shutterstock: 6-7, 16. Stock Connection Distribution/ Alamy: 20-
21, 23. ticktock Media Archive: 12, 13b. Max Tremlett: 4b. Roy Westwood: 7t, 8t, 8b, 9, 11 both.

Every effort has been made to trace copyright holders, and we apologise in advance for any omissions. We would be pleased to
insert the appropriate acknowledgments in any subsequent edition of this publication.

CONTENTS

GONE FISHING

Fishing is more than just catching fish. It's the anticipation of the bite. It's watching wildlife while you wait. It's enjoying the outdoors and the fresh air.

Coarse fishing is catching fish such as carp, pike and catfish from lakes and rivers.

Carp

Flies

Fly fishing is catching fish using imitation baits called flies.

Sea fishing is
catching fish,
such as bass,
from a beach
or from rocks.

Sea fishing can also
be catching big
game fish, such as
marlin, shark or tuna,
from a boat.

Sea fishing for bass

COARSE FISHING

There are two main ways of coarse fishing – using floats and legering.

Floats are used to present a bait between the lake bed and the surface.

Big carp hide in weeds at the edges of the lake.

Float

Predatory fish, such as pike, zander, perch and catfish like shelter. They hide in snag trees and reeds.

Tench and crucian carp like to hide under lily pads.

Lots of different baits can be used for coarse fishing –

- Worms and maggots
- Bread, cheese and sweetcorn
- Specially made boilies

Boilies

Legering uses a weight to keep the bait in one place on the bottom of the lake.

Bream feed on flat, weed-free areas such as behind gravel bars.

Weight

A DAY ON THE BANK

Today, I'm fishing a lake for carp. I have seen some carp jumping at one end.

I cast to where the fish are showing.

My bait is inside a PVA bag of feed pellets.

The bag will dissolve and leave the pellets on the lake bottom. They will attract the carp to my bait.

Bite alarm

The line runs through an electronic bite alarm. When a fish pulls the line, it sets off the alarm.

**After a few hours,
the alarm goes off.**

It's a carp!

The clutch on my
reel is set properly.
This allows the
fish to take line.
A carp can take
50 metres of line
from the reel when
it is first hooked.

CARING FOR THE CATCH

Coarse fish are usually put back into the water after capture. Other anglers can then enjoy catching them.

Always use a landing net to land the fish.

Keep the fish out of the water just long enough to unhook, weigh and photograph the fish.

Landing net

It is important that fish go back into the water in the same condition as when you caught them.

Unhooking mat

Big fish should be laid on a padded unhooking mat while you unhook them.

If you don't want to release the fish straight away, you can keep it in a keepnet for a short time.

Keepnet

A keepnet should be properly spread out.
It should be put in deep water in the shade.

LURES

Lures are a great way to catch predatory fish such as pike, zander and bass.

A lure is made from metal or plastic. It is shaped and painted so that it looks like a real fish.

Plugs look the most real. They are ideal in clear water for wary fish.

You can use a special lure rod with your lures. A lure rod has an action that makes the lure look like a real fish as it moves through the water.

Different lures attract different fish. Always carry a selection so you can try different ones.

Spoons reflect the light as they wobble through the water.

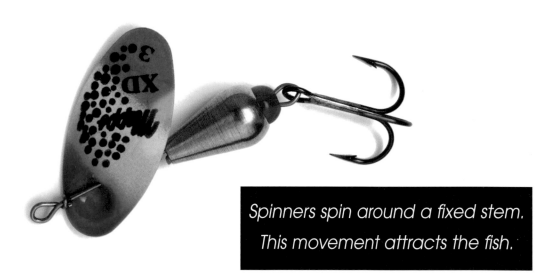

Spinners spin around a fixed stem. This movement attracts the fish.

Lures are great for short fishing sessions. You can keep lots of lures ready to go at any time!

Lure bag

FLY FISHING

Fly fishing is one way to catch fish such as trout and salmon. Anglers use flies, a long, responsive rod, a reel, and line.

This Atlantic salmon was caught using a fly. The water was so clear that the angler was able to spot the fish and cast the fly directly to it.

FLY FISHING - CASTING

To make a basic fly fishing cast, grip the rod as if you are shaking someone's hand. Pull as much line as you think you need off the reel. This will sit in a pile at your feet.

Think of your casting arm as a clock's hour hand.

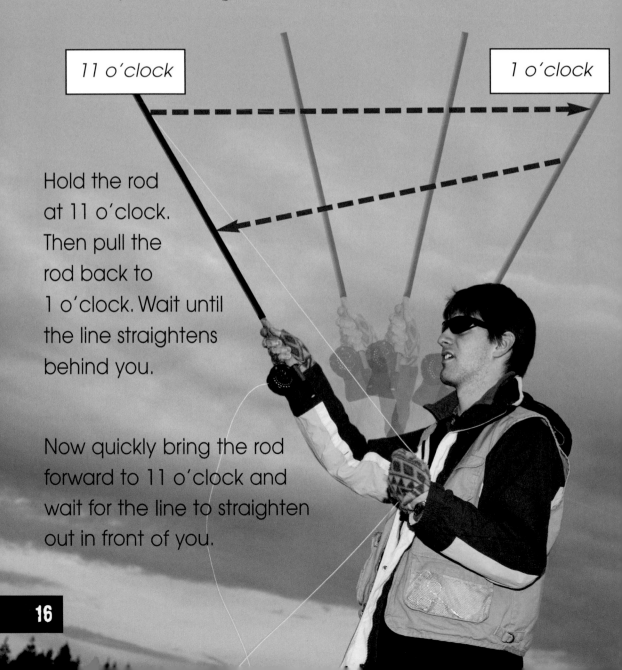

11 o'clock

1 o'clock

Hold the rod at 11 o'clock. Then pull the rod back to 1 o'clock. Wait until the line straightens behind you.

Now quickly bring the rod forward to 11 o'clock and wait for the line to straighten out in front of you.

Keep working the rod backwards and forwards.
As you do, allow more and more line out
through your fingers.

When your line is long enough to reach your
target, let the fly drop onto the water.

FLIES AND GEAR

Flies look like the insects that the fish eat. They are made from fur, feathers and thread tied onto a sharp hook.

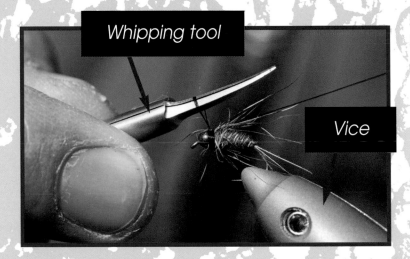

Whipping tool

Vice

Tying flies is very fiddly! But it's great to catch a fish with a fly you've tied yourself.

Fly fishing anglers wear vests with lots of pockets for storing gear such as fly boxes and sunglasses.

They also wear long, rubber boots or all-in-one boots and trousers. These are known as waders.

Vest

Waders

Net

Gold-ribbed hare's ear

Pheasant tail

Adams

Parachute Adams

Royal wulff

Elk hair caddis

Blue-winged olive

Compara dun olive

Sparkle dun

Muddler minnow

Olive woolly bugger

Black woolly bugger

The fly choice depends on which insects the fish are eating at that time of year.

Blue marlin can swim at **80 km/h.**

Some sea anglers like to fish for big game fish such as marlin, tuna and shark. This type of sea fishing is known as big game fishing.

Marlin are large, powerful fish. This makes them difficult to catch.

The largest ever blue marlin caught on a rod and reel weighed over 460 kilograms!

CATCHING A MARLIN

Big game fishing is done from a boat. Anglers can charter a boat with an experienced crew.

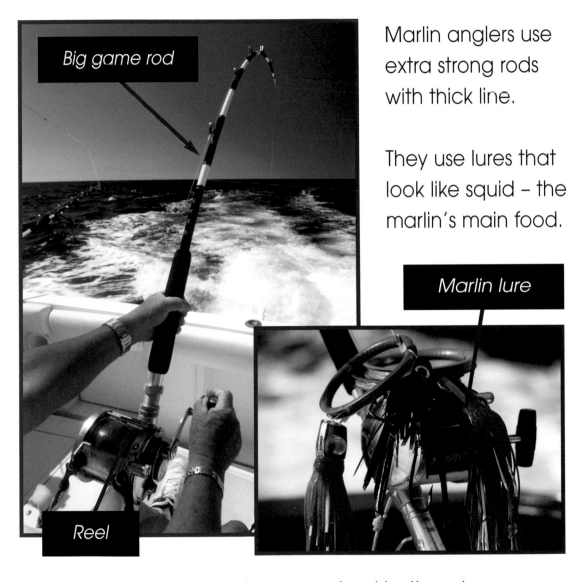

Big game rod

Reel

Marlin lure

Marlin anglers use extra strong rods with thick line.

They use lures that look like squid – the marlin's main food.

Anglers can also use natural bait, such as mackerel, combined with a lure. These are called "skirted baits".

Marlin can be found in warm oceans in places such as the Caribbean, South America, Africa, Australia and New Zealand.

A string of teasers is pulled behind the boat. This is known as trolling. The main lure is on the end, so it is first to be hit by the marlin.

Charter boat

Main lure

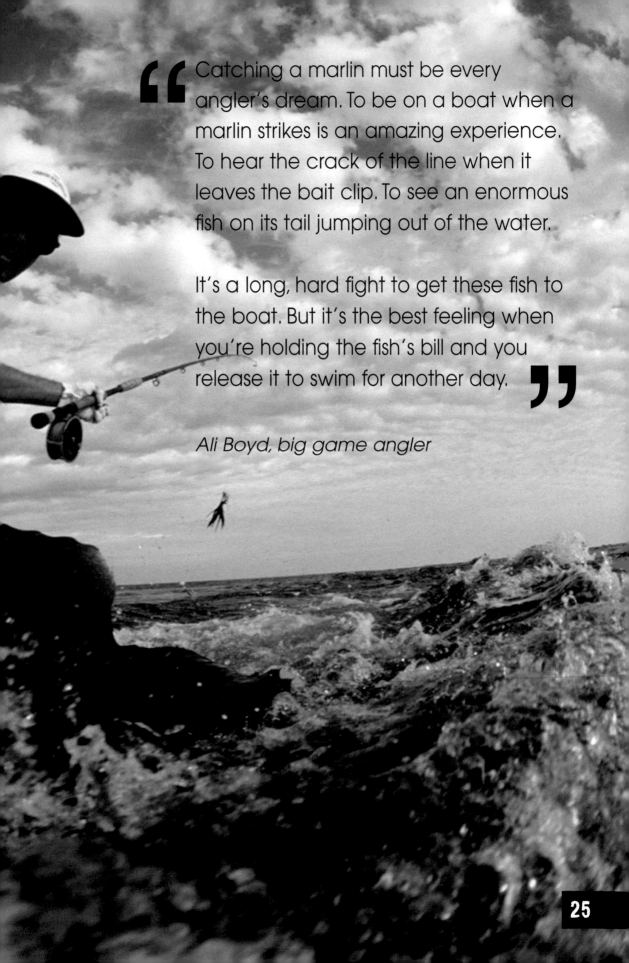

"Catching a marlin must be every angler's dream. To be on a boat when a marlin strikes is an amazing experience. To hear the crack of the line when it leaves the bait clip. To see an enormous fish on its tail jumping out of the water.

It's a long, hard fight to get these fish to the boat. But it's the best feeling when you're holding the fish's bill and you release it to swim for another day."

Ali Boyd, big game angler

MATCH FISHING

The World Match Fishing Championships is the most important competition for many anglers because they represent their country.

The championship is held in a different country each year. Teams from all over the world enter. Each team has five anglers.

A lake or river is split into five sections. One angler from each country fishes each section.

It doesn't matter how many fish you catch or what size they are. Your total weight of fish at the end of the two days is what counts.

There is a team gold medal to be won as well as an individual gold.

The 2007 championships in Hungary

CHAMPION ANGLER

British angler Alan Scotthorne has won the individual gold medal five times.

Even the smallest fish can make the difference between losing the match, or winning a gold medal for your country.

Alan at the 2007 championships in Hungary

" I've been fishing since I was six. My dream was just
to get into the England team.

The first time I won was in Italy. It was unbelievable!
Italy had a strong team so it was great to beat
them at home. We go as a team, so the team gold
is the most important. "

Alan Scotthorne

*Winning a fifth gold
medal in Hungary 2007*

" The best feeling was winning individual and
team gold in Croatia in 1998, and having two
gold medals around my neck! "

Alan Scotthorne

NEED TO KNOW WORDS

angler A person who catches fish using a rod and line.

anticipation Looking forward to something.

bait Food used to tempt fish.

bait clip A piece of equipment that holds the line in place. When a fish takes, it releases the line.

bill A long, pointed, bony snout.

bite When a fish takes the bait.

boilie A specially made fishing bait. Boilies are balls of paste with different flavours. They can be bought from fishing tackle shops.

charter To hire a boat and its crew.

clutch Part of a fishing reel. It allows line to be pulled off the spool by a fish. Without a clutch, your line would snap.

coarse fishing Catching fish, such as carp and pike, in lakes and rivers.

imitation Something that looks like, or pretends to be, something else.

land To bring a fish to land.

landing net A net with soft mesh for landing a fish.

predatory The word to describe an animal that hunts and eats other animals.

responsive Something that responds well. A responsive rod will make the actions you need quickly and accurately.

strikes Another word for a fish taking the bait (see bite).

teaser A lure or piece of bait that is used to attract a fish, but which doesn't have a hook.

CATCHING A RECORD

There are two types of records for anglers – national records and IGFA records.

see http://www.igfa.org/

- If you catch a record-breaking fish, you will need someone to witness your catch. Another angler is best.

- Weigh the fish in front of your witness. Contact the record-keeping organisation to let them know.

- Get your scales checked to make sure they are accurate. Fill out the claim form!

An IGFA record-breaking 15lb 12oz largemouth bass. It was caught by 11-year-old Mackenzie Ruth Hickox.

FISHING ONLINE

Websites

http://www.nfadirect.com

http://www.salmon-trout.org

http://www.a-c-a.org/

INDEX